Squirrels

Victoria Blakemore

vblakemore.author@gmail.com

Copyright info/picture credits

Cover, seawhisper/Shutterstock; Page 3, Pexels/Pixabay; Page 5, zoosnow/Pixabay; Page 7, CarinaHofi/Pixabay; Page 9, GIS/ Pixabay; Pages 10-11, Eléonore H/AdobeStock; Page 13, tom/ AdobeStock; Page 15, CreativePassion/Pixabay; Page 17, skeeze/Pixabay; Page 19, irishka5/Shutterstock; Page 21, citikka/AdobeStock; Page 23; ChmpagnDave/AdobeStock; Page 25, Alexas_Fotos/Pixabay; Page 27, Pexels/Pixabay; Page 29, silkebr/Pixabay; Page 31, klimkin/Pixabay; Page 33, seawhisper/Shutterstock

Table of Contents

What Are Squirrels?

Squirrels are a special kind of mammal called a rodent. They are related to other rodents such as chipmunks.

There are over 200 different kinds of squirrels. They differ in their color, size, and where they live.

There are three main types of squirrels: tree squirrels, ground squirrels, and flying squirrels.

Size

The smallest squirrel is the African pygmy squirrel. It can be between three and five inches long. It weighs less than an ounce.

The largest squirrel is the Indian giant squirrel. It can grow to be three feet long and weigh up to four pounds.

Many squirrels are between one and two feet long. They often weigh less than two pounds.

Physical Characteristics

Squirrels have a long, bushy tail. It can be used to help them balance. They can also wrap it around their body to stay warm.

Flying squirrels have a layer of skin between their front and back legs. This allows them to glide on the air.

Squirrels have paws that can

grasp and hold onto things.

They use them for climbing,

eating, and gathering food.

Habitat

Squirrels are able to **adapt** to living in many different habitats. They are often found in forests, prairies, rainforests, and even deserts.

Many squirrels also live in cities and towns. Some get into buildings and make their nests in attics.

Range

Squirrels are found on every

continent except Antarctica.

The Eastern gray squirrel is the most common squirrel. It is found in parts of North America.

Diet

Squirrels are **omnivores**. They eat both meat and plants.

Some squirrels eat leaves, nuts, roots, bark, and seeds. Other kinds of squirrels also eat small animals and insects, such as lizards, caterpillars, snakes, and bird eggs.

Squirrels have strong front teeth that never stop growing. This is important because they gnaw on things like nuts, so their teeth can wear down.

Many squirrels gather lots of extra food. They bury the extra food to keep it safe. They dig it up to eat when it is winter and food is harder to find.

Squirrels eat about one pound of food each week. It is important for them to put away plenty of food for the winter so they don't starve.

Squirrels have to watch for

predators like hawks, owls,

raccoons, and snakes. They

often run in zig-zags so that they

are harder to catch.

Communication

Squirrels use sound, scent, and movement to communicate with each other. They use their tail to signal if there is danger nearby.

They use their sense of smell to find other squirrels. They can make sounds like chirps, squawks, and alarm calls.

Squirrels are very **alert** animals.

They are always watching and

listening for predators.

Movement

Many squirrels can run at speeds of up to about twelve miles per hour. This is quite fast for a small animal.

Squirrels have sharp claws and **double-jointed** legs. This makes them great climbers. They are able to climb up and down trees very quickly.

Squirrels are able to leap long distances. They often leap from tree to tree.

Squirrel Kits

Squirrels usually have between two and eight babies. Their babies are called kits.

Kits are born blind and with very thin fur. Their fur grows in thicker as they get older. Kits are able to feed themselves by the time they are about ten weeks old.

Kits stay with their mother for the

first few months of their lives.

Their mother takes care of them.

Squirrel Life

Some squirrels are **solitary**. They prefer to live alone. Other squirrels live in groups that are called a dray or scurry.

Some squirrels **hibernate** during the winter. They sleep for long periods of time. This helps them to use less energy when less food is available.

Tree squirrels build nests in holes of tree trunks with branches, leaves and moss. Squirrels like ground squirrels dig burrows under the ground.

Squirrels as Pests

Squirrels are known for getting into attics. When they do, they build nests and can make a big mess.

They can also cause problems with electrical wires and telephone wires. This causes many people to think of squirrels as pests.

Squirrels can be very clever.

They can get into many kinds of

bird feeders to get the seeds

and nuts.

Population

Most squirrel populations are **stable** in the wild. There are thirteen kinds of squirrels that are **endangered**. They could soon become extinct.

The Namdapha flying squirrel is **critically endangered**. There are very few left in the wild.

In the wild, squirrels often live

between four and ten years.

Some may live as long as twenty.

Squirrels in Danger

The squirrels that are **endangered** are facing several threats. The main threat to many squirrels is habitat destruction.

In some places, new squirrels have been brought in. These new squirrels **compete** with **native** squirrels for food and territory.

The squirrelpox **virus** can make some squirrels very sick. Some squirrels can carry the virus without getting sick. They spread it to other squirrels.

Helping Squirrels

In the United Kingdom, many groups are working to help red squirrels. They are working to provide new habitats and increase their population.

In some places, protected areas have been set up. They provide animals like squirrels with a safe habitat.

Some groups work to help squirrels that are sick or hurt. They take care of them until they can be released back into the wild.

Researchers are studying squirrels. They want to help squirrels that are **native** to certain areas to survive the invasion of new squirrels.

Glossary

Adapt: to change

Alert: watching carefully

Compete: to try to get something others are trying to get

Critically Endangered: when an animal is almost extinct

Double-Jointed: having joints that bend at unusual angles

Endangered: at risk of becoming extinct

Hibernate: when an animal sleeps during the winter to use less energy

Native: an animal that has always lived in a certain place

Omnivore: an animal that eats meat and plants

Predator: an animal that hunts other animals for food

Solitary: living alone

Stable: not changing

Virus: a tiny organism that can make people or animals sick

Victoria Blakemore is a first grade

teacher in Southwest Florida with a

passion for reading.

You can visit her at

www.elementaryexplorers.com

Also in This Series

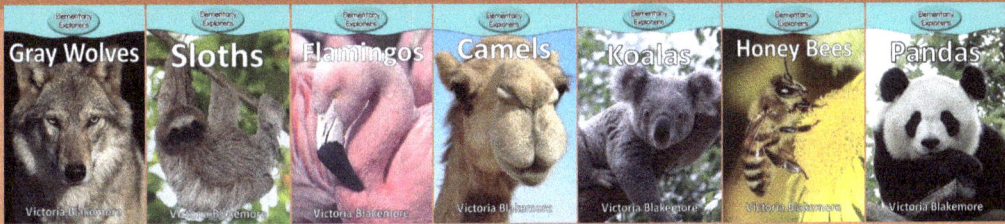

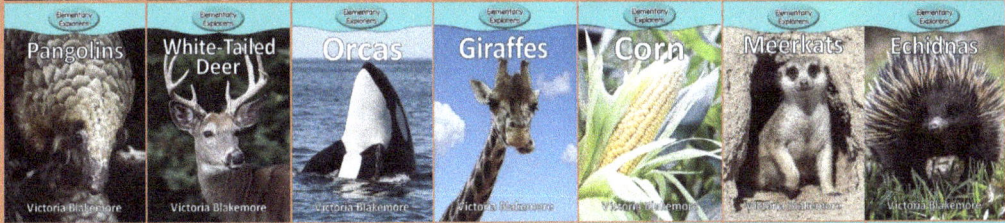

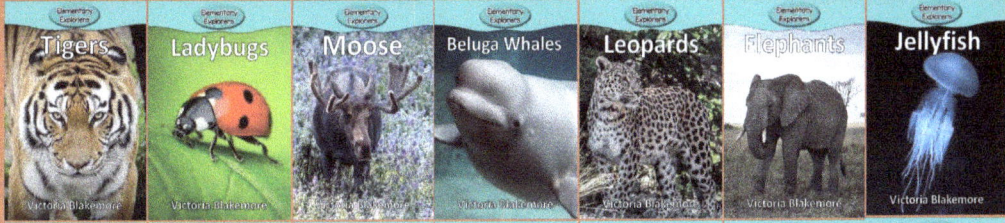

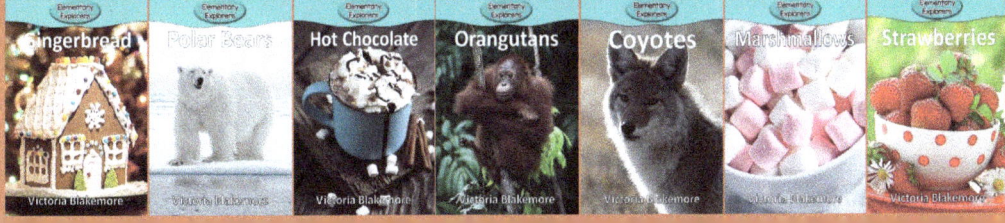

Gray Wolves	Sloths	Flamingos	Camels	Koalas	Honey Bees	Pandas
Pangolins	White-Tailed Deer	Orcas	Giraffes	Corn	Meerkats	Echidnas
Walruses	Raccoons	Bald Eagles	Apples	Arctic Foxes	Red Pandas	Cassowaries
Tigers	Ladybugs	Moose	Beluga Whales	Leopards	Elephants	Jellyfish
Binturongs	Lions	Dolphins	Reindeer	Hammerhead Sharks	Hippos	Pumpkins
Peafowl	Chameleons	Florida Panthers	Aye-Ayes	Black Bears	Cheetahs	Manatees
Gingerbread	Polar Bears	Hot Chocolate	Orangutans	Coyotes	Marshmallows	Strawberries

Victoria Blakemore

Also in This Series

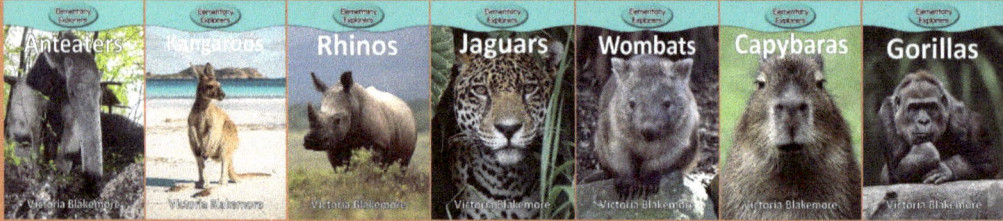

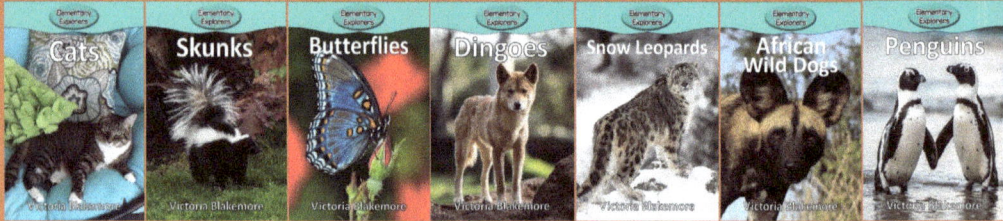

Aardvarks · Mako Sharks · Alligators · Frogs · Hedgehogs · Brown Bears · Bongos

Sea Turtles · Quokkas · Muskrats · Zebras · Red Foxes · Ring-Tailed Lemurs · Platypuses

Anteaters · Kangaroos · Rhinos · Jaguars · Wombats · Capybaras · Gorillas

Cats · Skunks · Butterflies · Dingoes · Snow Leopards · African Wild Dogs · Penguins

Whale Sharks · Wolverines · Warthogs · Caracals · Badgers · Seals · Hummingbirds

Pikas · Humpback Whales · Pumas · Lemonade · Llamas · Tulips · Ostriches

Sunflowers · Fennec Foxes · Sea Lions · Squirrels

Victoria Blakemore

www.ingramcontent.com/pod-product-compliance
Lightning Source LLC
Chambersburg PA
CBHW051254020426

42333CB00025B/3200